First Edition

Genuine Autographed Collectible

Do you want me to sign it in ink or in lipstick?

Love You More Than Yesterday

Date:

To:

From:

Message:

What Do Books Do?
BOOKS ARE POWERFUL

Books Educate
Books Enlighten
Books Empower
Books Entertain
Books Emancipate
Books Spring Eternal
Books Drive Exploration
Books Spark Evolution
Books Ignite Revolution

Sharon Esther Lampert

Gift Shop: BooksArePowerful.com

LYMTY

LOVE YOU MORE THAN YESTERDAY

14 Relationship Strategies for Happily Ever After!

MIND BODY SPIRIT BOOT CAMP

KADIMAH PRESS
Gifts of Genius

Self-Help, Psychology, Relationships, Sex, Romance, Love, Marriage, Marriage Counseling

LYMTY Love You More Than Yesterday
14 Relationship Strategies for Happily Ever After

©2022 First Edition by Sharon Esther Lampert. All Rights Reserved. No part of this book may be used or reproduced in any manner whatsoever without written permission except in the case of brief quotations embodied in critical articles and reviews.

KADIMAH PRESS GIFTS OF GENIUS

KADIMAH PRESS books may be purchased for education, business, or sales promotional use.

ISBN Hardcover: 978-1-885872- 28-9
ISBN E-Book: 978-1-885872- 27-2
Library of Congress Catalog Card Number: 2021900003

Author Website and Email:
FANS@SharonEstherLampert.com
www.SharonEstherLampert.com

Editor: Dave Segal

Cover and Interior Book Design: Creative Genius Sharon Esther Lampert
Publisher: www.PalmBeachBookPublisher.com
Phone: 917-767-5843
Email: Sharon@PalmBeachBookPublisher.com

To Order Book:
Ingram, 1 Ingram Blvd. La Vergne, TN 37086-3629
Phone: 615-793-5000
Fax orders: 615-287-6990

First Edition
Manufactured in the United States of America

Age 9:
THE QUEEN HAS ARRIVED!
"My daughter is a poet, philosopher, and teacher. Sharon is the Princess & the Pea!
BEAUTY & BRAINS!"
MOMMY
XOXO

Dedication
To My Muses

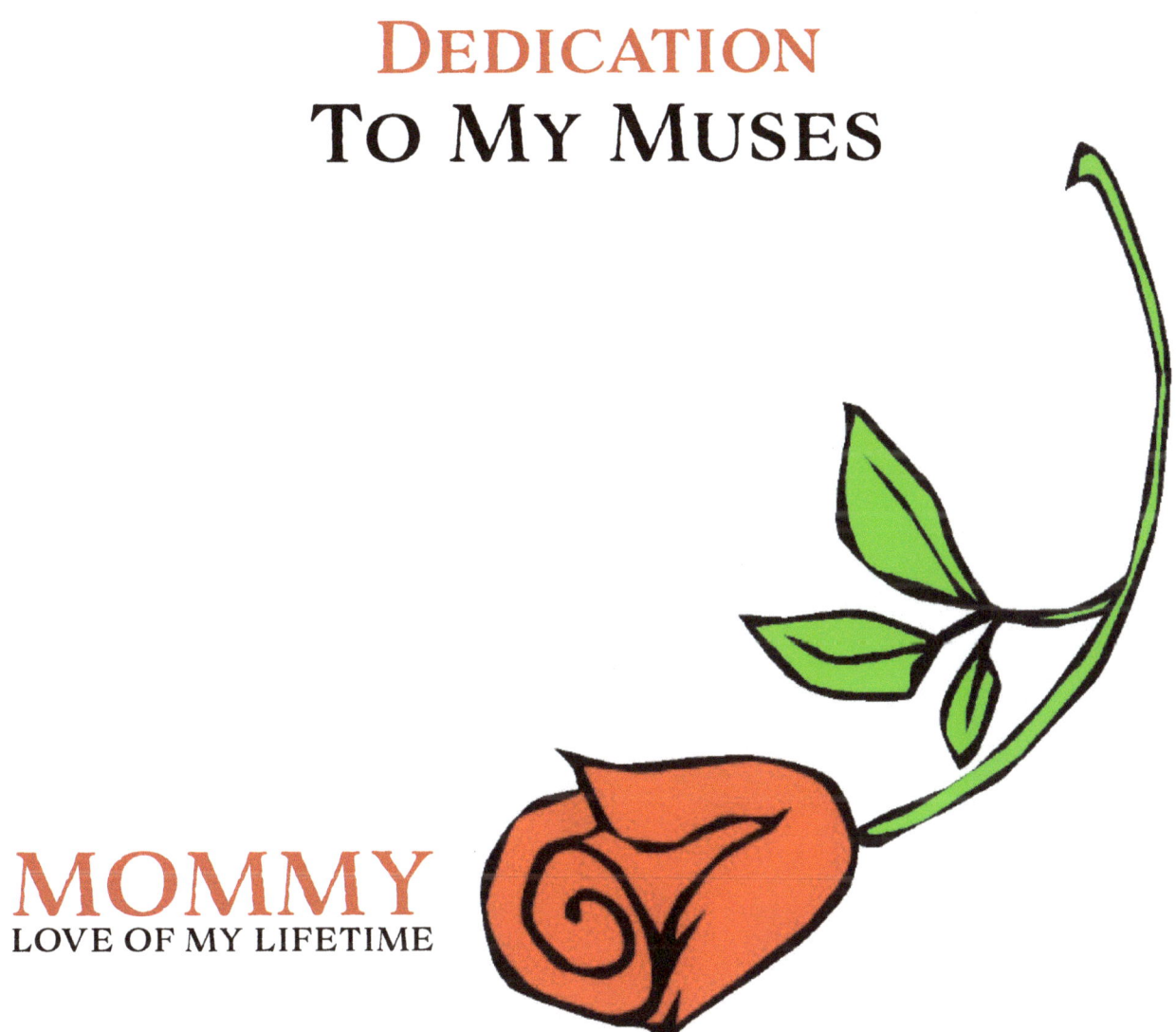

MOMMY
LOVE OF MY LIFETIME

TRUE LOVE

True Love is Unconditional.
True Love is Found in the Deed.
True Love is Found in the We.
True Love Unites the Mind,
Body, and Heart as One.

Sharon Esther Lampert

TABLE OF CONTENTS

14 Relationship Strategies for Happily Ever After!

1. **ME:** The Most Important Relationship p. 1
2. **WE:** Bonus Love p. 3
3. Prospects Not Projects p. 5
4. You Don't Find Love, You Create Love p. 7
5. Each Day is a Fresh Start p. 9
6. Soundbites of Respectful Communication p. 11
7. **TEAMWORK:** Divide & Conquer p. 13
8. No 3rd Parties Allowed p. 15
9. Negotiate a Great Deal: **WIN! WIN!** p. 17
10. Daily Life Tests and Lessons Learned p. 19
11. Practice Gratitude Over Grievances p. 21
12. Don't Go Through It — Grow Through It! p. 23
13. Metamorphosis p. 25
14. **LIVE YOUR TRUTH** p. 27

Love Quotes pp. 29-32

Love Poetry pp. 33-35

About the Author pp. 36-37

Gifts of Genius pp. 38-39

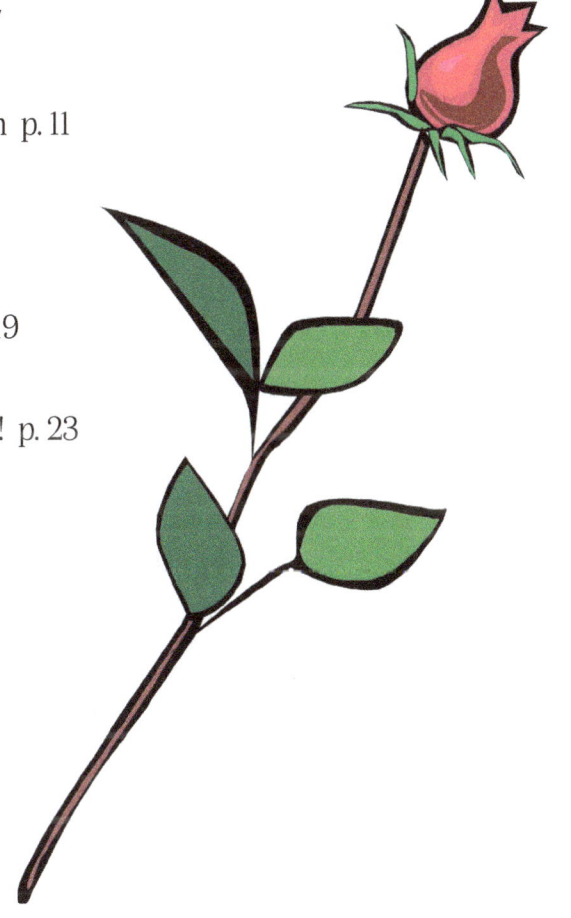

LOVE NOTES TO SELF   SELFCARE IS NOT SELFISH!

Rule 1. ME Is Your Most Important Relationship!
How fortunate we are to be living in a world of unlimited opportunities!

My Day! My Dream! My Destiny!
You can transform your mind, body and spirit to live your **BEST LIFE!**

Nurture Mind, Body, and Spirit!
- Mind: Education, Enlightenment & Empowerment
- Body: Health, Exercise & Energy
- Spirit: Meditation, Mindfulness, Mantra & Music

"**M**editation, **M**indfulness, **M**antra, and **M**usic **M**itigates MADNESS!"

—Philosopher Queen Sharon Esther Lampert

Birth Bubble
We start from a place where everything is decided for us: family, culture, language, country, and education. At some point in our timelines, we are exposed to the greater world outside of our birth bubble. If we want to, we can change almost everything: name, language, home, friends, and career. We can start a new chapter in life, and live our lives based on our personal preferences — not based on childhood social conditioning.

Life Is Lived First by Default — Later by Design
Break Out of Your Birth Bubble and Live Your Best Life!

Rule 1

SELf LOVE

The Most Important Relationship Is The One You Have with Yourself

How Is That Going?

Mind
Body
Spirit

LOVE NOTES TO SELF

Rule 2. BONUS LOVE: ME to WE

People come into our lives for a reason, a season or a lifetime! Why is this person in my life at this moment in time?

Start Asking and Answering Questions:
Q. Is there an intimate **Connection?**
Q. Is there **Chemistry?**
Q. Is there respectful **Communication?**
Q. Is there **Compatibility?**
Q. Is there **Common Ground?**
Q. Are we on a similar **Frequency?** Shared Values? Shared Goals?
Q. Are there any **Red Flags?** _____

"A Warm Nobody is Better Than a Cold Somebody!"

—Philosopher Queen Sharon Esther Lampert

We Are Born Alone and We Die Alone

Every life story is unique and has a beginning, a middle, and an end! From cradle to grave, we meet people along the way — a select few become memorable. Often, our beloved pets are even more cherished than the people in our lives, because they offer us unconditional love.

Rule 2

Love from Outside of Yourself Is
BONUS LOVE
ME PLAN to WE PLAN

Date Night Strategy
1. Bring a gift.
2. Make a toast & propose:
   "Friends First & Forever!"
3. Send "Thank You" note.
4. Repeat!

LOVE NOTES TO SELF

Rule 3. Prospects Not Projects

Prospects Long-Term Relationships

Relationships are constructive associations. Relationships energize, inspire, and support.

Q. Is there a possibility for a life-long relationship based on mutual respect, empathy, understanding, and love?

In Sum: LOVE STORY Is a WIN! WIN!

Projects: Smart% + Stupid% + Sick%

This kind of relationship turns every encounter into a therapy session. These therapy sessions reveal an **undiagnosed** mental disorder, and unresolved childhood family trauma.

Projects are drowning in negative energy! The glass is half empty!

Projects need full-time psychiatrists. This is draining, exhausting, and you will burn out!

Projects need therapy sessions from professionals — not from you!

Projects have undiagnosed genetic mental disorders, e.g., Bipolar Disorder.

In Sum: LOVE STORY Is a WIN! LOSE! or a LOSE! LOSE!

Rule 3

Prospects Not Projects

LOVE NOTES TO SELF

Rule 4. You Don't Find Love, You Create Love

What Is Love? Kindness, Respect, Patience, Understanding, Empathy, and Compassion.

TRUE LOVE IS UNCONDITIONAL LOVE
Unconditional Love Is Real — But Rare!
You can never know another person:
- You marry a stranger.
- You have sex with a stranger.
- You have children with a stranger.

"All People Help You with Their Strengths and Hurt You with Their Weaknesses."

—Philosopher Queen Sharon Esther Lampert

Here is a Recipe to Create Love
- Part Empathy
- Part Understanding
- Part Validation
- Part Unconditional
- Part Respect
- Part Tolerance

What is your recipe for LOVE?

"There Is No Such Thing as Too Much Love!"

—Philosopher Queen Sharon Esther Lampert

Rule 4

You Don't Find Love
YOU CREATE LOVE

LOVE NOTES TO SELF

Rule 5. Daily Fresh Start

Leave your personal baggage in a dumpster:
- Childhood Baggage
- Family Baggage
- Relationship Baggage
- Work Baggage
- Cultural Baggage
- Religious Baggage

"50% of People are Trying to GET INTO a Relationship, and the Other 50% of People are Trying to GET OUT of a Relationship!"

—Philosopher Queen Sharon Esther Lampert

Every Day Is A Fresh Start:
- Practice Mindfulness — Be Present in the Moment!
- Practice Meditation — Clear Your Mind of Negative Thoughts!
- Let Go of Yesterday — You Can't Right the Wrongs of the Past!
- Keep a Journal and Record Feelings — Maintain Relationship to Self

EVERYONE MAKES MISTAKES!
Games are won and lost by the team that made fewer mistakes!
The learning curve is steep — most couples fail their way to success!

Rule 5

Each Day is a Fresh Start
Choose a **Fresh Start** Over Righting the Wrongs of the Past
You Can't Unbake a Cake!
Forget the Mistake!
Remember the Lesson!

LOVE NOTES TO SELF

Rule 6. Respectful Communication

Learn how to listen to a loved one without judgement or offering advice. Apply endless patience, empathy, understanding, and **MIRROR** back words said.

1. Be Present   2. Pause   3. Paraphrase

Most of the time, having a toolbox of respectful soundbites is a safe and effective way to not say the wrong thing at the wrong time.

Here is a small sampling of soundbites that will come in handy for family, friends, and strangers:

"Tell me more…"   "I hear you!"   "Is that true?"

"Thank you for sharing"   "I feel your pain!"   "I'm here for you!"

"Are you doing the best you can under the circumstances?"

LUVU

LOVE, UNDERSTAND, VALIDATE, UNCONDITIONAL.

Rule 6

Respectful Communication
Use Soundbites to Create Safe Zones
to Share Honest Communication
"Thank you for sharing"
"Tell me more…"
"I'm sorry!"

LOVE NOTES TO SELF

Rule 7. Teamwork: WE Plan

Life is labor intensive, and humanity is interconnected by service. Service is an act of organized collaboration known as teamwork. Take into account your own strengths and weaknesses and delegate responsibilities accordingly — for small insignificant stuff, larger critical tasks, and overwhelming vicissitudes of life.

DO, DOING (DIY or DELEGATE), DONE

DIY: Divide & Conquer

Q. What are your strengths and weaknesses?
Q. What are your likes and dislikes?
   Separate chores into two lists or do them together as one.
   Take turns doing the chores, "It's your turn to get the car washed!"

Delegate: Hire Professionals

Stop fighting over this, that, and the other! Bring in professionals to help you get small stuff, medium size stuff, and big stuff done.

Rule 7

Teamwork
Strengths and Weaknesses

Opposites Don't Attract, They Attack!

**Divide & Conquer
DIY or Delegate to Professionals**

LOVE NOTES TO SELF

Rule 8. Relationships Are a Private Party

Make a Pack to Keep Your Private Life Private!
Don't chit chat with family, friends, and coworkers about your private life. Only speak to professionals who abide by confidentiality protocol. **NO OVERSHARING!**

Keep a Daily Journal to Process Your Feelings
"Get in Front of the Problem Before the Problem Gets in Front of You!"

—Philosopher Queen Sharon Esther Lampert

WARNING: Unresolved personal baggage is toxic — and will destroy your relationship — END OF LOVE STORY!

Warning! No Behind the Back Bashing and Throwing Lover Under Bus! — END OF LOVE STORY!

Schedule Monthly Checkups
Most people marry a **STRANGER**, and only become familiar with the **STRANGER** after marriage, a few kids, a deed to a house, and a pet. Go for monthly relationships checkups — similar to giving your car a regular car wash, because cookie crumbs are hiding inside the car seats.

Rule 8

Relationships Are a Private Party
NO THIRD PARTIES ALLOWED!

No Behind the Back Bashing
No Throwing Lover Under the Bus!

NO OVERSHARING!

LOVE NOTES TO SELF

Rule 9. Negotiate a Great Deal

LOVE is a series of transactional exchanges. How do you negotiate a great deal with a **WIN! WIN!** outcome for both parties?

Time:
Q. How much together time? How much alone time?

Money:
Q. How much money will be spent for this, that, and the other?

Sharing:
Q. What is shared property, and what belongs to each of you?

Childrearing:
Caretaking responsibilities are no longer dictated soley by traditional gender stereotypes. Whose turn is it to take the kids to and from school?

Prenuptial:
Q. Who gets the dog, a member of the family after the divorce?

Rule 9

Negotiate a Great Deal!
WIN! WIN!

LOVE NOTES TO SELF

Rule 10. Daily Lessons Learned

Q. What are you learning about yourself?

Q. What are you learning about each other?

Q. Do you want to go in the same direction?

Q. Do you want to go in different directions?

Q. Are you growing together or growing apart?

The Learning Curve Is Steep! Creating New Habits Takes Time.
New Habit: 30 Days   **Practice:** 60 Days   **New Normal:** 90 Days

Q. Are you able to meet your own needs?

Q. Are you helping each other meet each other's needs?

Q. Are you different but complementary?

Q. What Works?   Q. What Doesn't Work?   Do What Works!

Rule 10

Daily Life Tests
Daily Lessons Learned

**Every Day You Will Take a Test.
What Test Did You Take Today?**

LOVE NOTES TO SELF

Rule 11. Practice Gratitude: Count You Blessings!

Gratitude is a spiritual tool to increase your happiness and joy!
I am grateful for: _____
I am grateful for: _____
I am grateful for: _____

"Find the Light and Live in the Light!"

—Philosopher Queen Sharon Esther Lampert

Let Go of Daily Grievances!

LIFE IS TEMPORARY INSANITY: PLANET! PROBLEMS! PEOPLE!
Stop complaining! Stop whining! Stop playing the victim! Life is unfair!

Practice Daily Gratitude with Poetic Gem

Count your **blessings** instead of your crosses;
Count your **gains** instead of your losses.

Count your **joys** instead of your woes;
Count your **friends** instead of your foes.

Count your **smiles** instead of your tears;
Count your **courage** instead of your fears.

Count your **full years** instead of your lean;
Count your **kind deeds** instead of your mean.

Count your **health** instead of your wealth;

—Author Unknown!

Rule 11

**Gratitude Over Grievances
Count Your Blessings!
Find the Light and
Live in the Light!**

LOVE NOTES TO SELF

Rule 12. Go Through It and Grow Through It!

There are speed bumps and curve balls:
Q. Is the curve ball a temporary frustration?
Q. Is the curve ball a chronic condition?
Q. Is the curve ball a permanent situation?

What Is a Catastrophe Curve Ball?

1. COVID19: Global Catastrophic Trauma!
2. Sudden onset of chronic-debilitating illness
3. Sudden death of a family member

1st Step: **Radical Acceptance of What Is!**
2nd Step: **Think Things Though, Take Action, Move Forward!**
3rd Step: **Evaluate Your Options!**

Evaluate Your Options:

Plan A. Let It Go!
Plan B. Learn to Live with It!
Plan C. Close One Chapter and Open New Chapter!
Plan D. Forgive — But Never Forget!
Plan E. Forgive and Forget!
Plan F. **Go Through It and Grow Through It!**

Rule 12

**Don't Go Through It!
Grow Through It!**

LOVE NOTES TO SELF

Rule 13. METAMORPHOSIS
The only constant in life is **CHANGE!** From the moment of conception, we are transforming in mind, body and spirit. We experience constant change without our consent or consideration. **LIFE HAPPENS!**

Every 5 Years, You Will Make a Life Transition

SELF: You cannot alter your **DNA** and your **GENETIC** disposition. Our own identities are in constant flux throughtout our lives: baby, toddler, child, teenager, young adult, adult, and senior citizen. There is growth, maturation, and development, and later regression and death.

Q. What contribution is this person making in my life?

Q. Am I a better person for having known this person?

Q. Are we stronger together?

Rule 13

METAMORPHOSIS
Become Better People for Knowing Each Other

LOVE NOTES TO SELF

Rule 14. BUILD 3 LIVES

Counterintuitively, your relationship will work better if you set up your lives for 3 lives instead of 2 lives:
1. My Life
2. Your Life
3. Our Life: WE Time & Shared Personal Space

3rd Life: Focus on your own goals, aspirations, ambitions, and dreams, and make a separate SPACE for SHARED endeavors.

SHARED SPACE: Meals, Family Celebrations, Holidays, Vacations

Plan in Place on Paper:
- Saturday nights is DATE NIGHT
- Sunday morning is BREAKFAST IN BED
- Sunday evening is ALONE TIME
- Wednesday evening is ALONE TIME
- M-F: BACK TO THE GRIND

Happily Married Couples All Say the Same Thing:
"I married my best friend!"

Rule 14

LIVE YOUR TRUTH

3 LIVES

**Mine
Yours
Ours**

"You Don't Marry Someone
You Can Live With.
You Marry the Person You
Cannot Live Without."
—Unknown

Love Quotes

"All That Matters In Life
Is Who You Love and
Who Loves You Back"

—Unknown

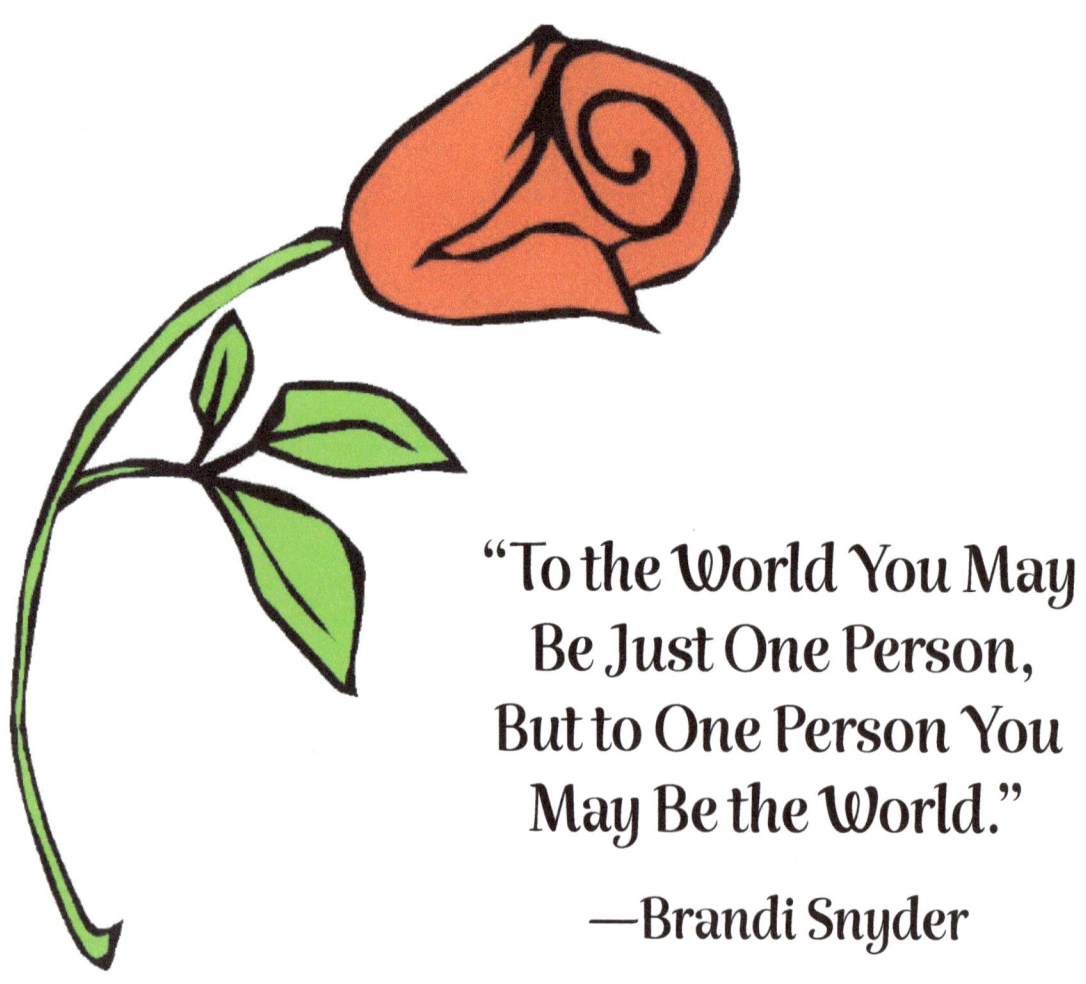

"To the World You May
Be Just One Person,
But to One Person You
May Be the World."

—Brandi Snyder

"I Don't Wish to Be
Everything to Everyone,
but I Would Like to Be
Something to Someone."

—Javan

Sivan Melody of F/Light

Dancing in his kitchen
To Cuban beats on a drum
Clothing falls to the floor, and
He sweeps me into the next door.

Making love in his arms
To Israeli rhythms on a heartbeat
Blankets fall to the floor, and
Passions are set free to pour.

Into the next day, as the music of
Love continues to play, a lovebird
Sitting on his sill, sings and sways, and
Waits for me to begin my day…

A cozy nest, a brief respite,
Before we again take flight,
Another day, another journey,
Encircling the sun, into the light.

—Sharon Esther Lampert
Book: "Sweet Nothings: 40 Love Poems"

Love Poetry

My Man
Making Love All Through the Night and All Through the Day

My Man is passionate and strong, all through
the night, I know his emotional,
spiritual, and physical being; I feel
the breadth and depth of his masculinity.

All through the night, My Man holds
me tightly in his arms: warm, tender,
and cuddly, childlike, always knowing
where I am, secure forevermore.

My Man's touch lingers,
I am sleeping soundly all
through the night, still making
love with him, in my dreams.

I awaken to My Man's soft kisses at
dawn, my spirit floating in the morning
mist, the promise of love is fulfilled,
my heart is murmuring a melody, a
sweet new song, all through the day.

—Sharon Esther Lampert
© WorldFamousPoems.com
© SharonEstherLampert.com
Book: "Sweet Nothings: 40 Love Poems"

THAT KISS

Fortune teller that I AM,
My crystal ball sees ALL.
Clairvoyant, the man's libido is flamBOYant.
I SEE: ANIMAL MAGNETISM.
Inside of THAT KISS will be bliss.

Taking chances with amorous glances
He advances... Lips pouting-tongue tied:
THAT KISS: SmOOch; smOOch.
When he romances: his gait prances,
his penis lances, his generosity enhances.
VOODOO, or DOO-YOU want dinner, dear?"
His heart dances....

Magician that he is
He has a loaded deck of cards
And wants to be my bodyguard.
Enchantment: a bag of mesmerizing tricks,
An ACE up his sleeve, a KING or a JACK
Are inside of his top hat of black.
Sleight of hand, THAT KISS is grand.

Wizardry: Pressed into his bosom
I am caught in his embraces, arms
Flailing, like a net above my head
His pounding heart is beating red.
THAT KISS tells ALL or just enough
to keep me Interested in ALL of his stuff.

Lips full of feelings, THAT KISS
Soft as rose petals, free of prickly thorns.
In the dark recesses of his mouth
I find my way by the light in his eyes
His smile is real, there is no disguise.

Even though we just met
I am caught in the tangled web of
A hot-blooded, Israeli-Englishman:
"A Jack of All of Love's Trades."
A rare mixed-breed, a British accent,
Concealing a *Sabra, wherever he went.
Tricks of my own trade, I roll up my sleeve,
And I become a woman-in-need(?)
THAT KISS I can't forget, and with no regret:
It is almost 4 a.m., and inside of my gypsy's tent:
Sm(OO)ch, sm(OO)ch
We are still one silhouette.

Animal Magetism:
Sm(OO)ch, sm(OO)ch,
Some call it v(OO)d(OO),
Most think it witchcraft,
Experts refer to it as "osculation."
Others call THAT KISS Kabbalah;
A kind of Jewish mysticism:
Many are in need of exorcism.

—Sharon Esther Lampert
©WorldFamousPoems.com
©SharonEstherLampert.com
Book: "Sweet Nothings: Love Poetry"

Sharon Esther Lampert

NYU
Honored Sharon Esther Lampert
with an Award for
"Multi-Interdisciplinary Studies"

Pro**d**i**g**y
Poet
Prophet
Philosopher
Peacemaker
Paladin of Education
Photon Superhero
Princess Kadimah
Pinup
Performer:Vocalist
Player:Jock
President
Publisher
Producer
Psychobiologist
Piano-Playing Cat
Phoenix

25 Websites:
- SharonEstherLampert.com
- WorldFamousPoems.com
- PoetryJewels.com
- VeryExtraSpecial.com
- PhilosopherQueen.com
- GodIsGoDo.com
- BooksArePowerful.com
- TrueLoveBurnsEternal.com
- SillyLittleBoys.com
- PalmBeachBookPublisher.com
- WritersRunTheWorld.com
- HappyGrandparenting.com

Education:
- PhotonSuperHero.com
- Smartgrades.com
- EveryDayAnEasyA.com
- BooksNotBombs.com

About the Author

Sharon Esther Lampert
V.E.S.S.E.L **V**ery. **E**xtra. **S**pecial. **S**haron. **E**sther. **L**ampert

PRODIGY
Unleash The Creator, The God Within: 10 Esoteric Laws of Genius & Creativity

POET
One of the World's Greatest Poets
POETRY WORLD RECORD: 120 WORDS OF RHYME
Greatest Poems Ever Written on Extraordinary World Events

PROPHET
- **22 COMMANDMENTS**: All You Will Ever Need To Know About God
- God Talks To Me: A Working Definition Of God GOD IS GO! DO!

PHILOSOPHER QUEEN
- Temporary In**s**anity: We Are Building Our Lives on a **S**and Trap — Written In Letter **S**
- Women Have All The Power But Have Never Learned How to Use It
- God of What? 11 Esoteric Laws of Inextricability
- Sperm Manifesto: 10 Rules For The Road

PEACEMAKER
WORLD PEACE EQUATION.com

PALADIN OF EDUCATION
PHOTON SUPERHERO
SMARTGRADES BRAIN POWER REVOLUTION
"The Silent Crisis Destroying America's Brightest Minds" — **BOOK OF THE MONTH, Alma Public Library, Wisconsin**

PIONEER
- Silly Little Boys: 40 Rules of Manhood, For Men of All Ages
- **C**upid: Language of Love — Written In Letter **C**
- **P**ublish: The Secret Sauce of Book Sales — Written In Letter **P**
- **D**estiny: Are You Living Life By **D**efault or By **D**esign?

PRINCESS KADIMAH
8TH PROPHETESS OF ISRAEL

PINUP
SEXIEST CREATIVE GENIUS IN HUMAN HISTORY

Sharon Esther Lampert

THANK YOU
Count Your Blessings and Gratitude

Blessing 1. My Genetic Gift of Genius — Lefty!
- Artistic Gifts Are Inherited: Painter Maternal Grandfather Benjamin Paikoff & Sculptor Father Abraham Lampert
- Vocalist: Ashira Orchestra, 18 Years: Ramaz Women's Service (YOUTUBE videos)
- Athlete: "Faster Than Any Boy, Anytime, Anywhere, Any Age!"

Blessing 2. My Life — Dawn of the Digital Revolution
- APPLE: The Golden Age of Personal Computers
- ADOBE: The Golden Age of Creativity
- INGRAM: The Golden Age of Publishing
- SOCIAL MEDIA: The Golden Age of the Internet & Global Communication
- iTUNES: The Golden Age of Music and Lyrics

Blessing 3. My Loved Ones:
- Self-Love: "Mindfulness, Meditation, and Music Mitigates MADNESS!"
- Unconditional Love: Mommy Eve Lampert
- My **PURR**fect Children: SCHMALTZY and FALAFEL, Schmaltzy.com
- My Muse Karl Bardosh "Friends First and Forever, and Family"
- My Spiritual Sister Poet Hannah Sezenes: "ELI, ELI"
- My Muses and N.Y.C. Night Life
- My Bubbe Esther Tulkoff, EstherTulkoff.com

NYU Professor Karl Bardosh and Me

Blessing 4. My Education, Educators and Awards
- NYU BA, MA, MA — NYU Award for Multi-Interdisciplinary Studies (YOUTUBE videos)
- NYU MENTOR Professor Laurin Raiken
- NYU "Multi-Interdisciplinary Award" and M.A. Class Representative at Graduation
- Rockefeller University, NYC — Publication: "Hyperphagia and Obesity Induced by Neuropeptide Y" — Laboratory of Dr. Sarah Leibowitz and Dr. Glen Stanley
- 100-Year Scholarship Award Winner, Presented by NYC Mayor Edward Koch
- Empire Science Scholarship Award Winner
- Jerusalem Fellowship Award, Aish Hatorah, Israel
- First Prize: Upper East Side Resident Writing Contest
- Egalitarian Education: Robert Gordis Solomon Schecter Day School

Blessing 5. My Sports
- NYC Marathon
- Basketball: NYU Women's Varsity Basketball Team, Center, Coach Sherri Pickard
- Basketball: NYC Urban Professional League, Guard
- Skiing: Heavenly, Lake Tahoe, Nevada
- Tennis: NYC Central Park Tennis Courts
- Weightlifting Contest Winner! NYU Coles Sports Center
- Basketball and Baseball, Coach Sandy Pyonin
- Basketball: Coaches Chicago Bulls Phil Jackson and Bill Walton
- Baseball: Coaches Baseball Hall of Fame Wilma Briggs and Jean Harding

NYU Professor Laurin Raiken and Me

Blessing 6. My Inspirations
- ISRAEL "AM YISRAEL CHAI!" LAMBS to SLAUGHTER to LIONS to LIGHT of the WORLD — Less Than 1% of Population and 22% of Nobel Prizes!
- NYC Personal Freedom and Creative Freedom
- USA Land of Possibility!

KADIMAH PRESS: Gifts of Genius

POETRY: 18 Books of Poetry
Title: I STOLE ALL THE WORDS FROM THE DICTIONARY
ISBN Hardcover: 978-1-885872-06-7
ISBN Paperback: 978-1-885872-07-4
ISBN E-Book: 978-1-885872-08-1
SharonEstherLampert.com

PROPHECY
**Title: THE 22 COMMANDMENTS:
ALL YOU WILL EVER NEED TO KNOW ABOUT GOD**
ISBN Hardcover: 978-1-885872-03-6
ISBN Paperback: 978-1-885872-04-3
ISBN E-Book: 978-1-885872-05-0
SharonEstherLampert.com

CHILDREN'S LITERATURE, Ages 7-13
Title: SCHMALTZY: IN AMERICA, EVEN A CAT CAN HAVE A DREAM
ISBN Hardcover: 978-1-885872-39-5
ISBN Paperback: 978-1-885872-38-8
ISBN E-Book: 978-1-885872-37-1
Schmaltzy.com

SELF-HELP
**Title: SILLY LITTLE BOYS: 40 RULES OF MANHOOD
HOW DO SILLY LITTLE BOYS GROW INTO SANE BIG MEN?**
ISBN Hardcover: 978-1-885872-29-6
ISBN Paperback: 978-1-885872-35-7
ISBN E-Book: 978-1-885872-41-8
SillyLittleBoys.com

COOKBOOK
**Title: SEX ON A PLATE: FOOD AS FOREPLAY
THE COOKBOOK OF EVERLASTING LOVE**
ISBN Hardcover: 978-1-885872-46-3
ISBN Paperback: 978-1-885872-48-7
ISBN E-Book: 978-1-885872-47-0
TrueLoveBurnsEternal.com

KADIMAH PRESS
Gifts of Genius

I Am Mortal.
My Books Are Immortal.
Please Handle My Books Gently.
My Books Are My Remains.

This book was compiled in three parts.
Part 1. Birth of Idea — 2014
Part 2. Format Book — 2021
Part 3. Publish Book — 2022

Sharon Esther Lampert
SEE THE WORLD THROUGH THE EYES OF A CREATIVE GENIUS
Poet, Prophet, Philosopher, Peacemaker, and Prodigy

www.ingramcontent.com/pod-product-compliance
Lightning Source LLC
Chambersburg PA
CBHW042354280426
43661CB00095B/1045